Beyond Chaos is a touching memoir about resilience, adaptability, humor and the power of the choice to heal and overcome. Debra's story is a shining example of how life's challenges and adversity are the very threads we weave to fulfill our life's work.

— *Sydney Culver*
Coach and Healer

In *Beyond Chaos,* we are given the privilege to witness Debra's flight from chaos to victory. She reminds us through her honesty and transparency that truth and an open heart always win. This book serves as an inspiration that we are never stuck in chaos and there's always a way through and beyond our setbacks. Thank you, Debra for this incredible gift.

— *Patrick Feren*
Spiritual Director, Center for Spiritual Living Kauai

Debra Valentina takes us on a rollercoaster ride through her life with unexpected twists and turns as she plays with time through her storytelling. With an open heart and a willingness to share her deepest shame and personal triumphs, she illustrates that anything is possible for each of us. Thank you, Debra, for your authenticity and the tools to rescue our own souls from chaos. *Beyond Chaos* is a great read for anyone ready to move from "I can't" to "Yes, I can!"

— *Rita Andriello-Feren*
Spiritual Director, Center for Spiritual Living Kauai

Debra takes readers on a journey into the depths of a chaotic childhood and shows us that sheer determination and grit will get you to the other side. Her straightforward, raw writing style feels like a one-two punch, then will have you cheering. *Beyond Chaos* is a lifeline of hope and inspiration, watching how one remarkable woman chose freedom and joy over victimhood, and is making the most of her life.

— Karen Gruber
Founder of The Inspired Mama

Beyond Chaos is an insightful story of perseverance, self-love and demonstrates the willingness to transcend life situations with utmost integrity and empowerment. Debra's story is confirmation that everything in life happens for a reason, and we are always at choice on how we take care of ourselves in all our relationships and experiences.

— Michelle LeMay
World-traveling minister-in-training

Everyone experiences chaos in their lives. The positive decisions and actions that some make after their experiences set them apart from most who choose to dwell in self-pity and despair. Despite the many challenges Debra shares from her life, her story serves as a guide to how we can rise as the phoenix from the ashes to become more joyous and fulfilled.

— Bill Baker, Ed.D.
Personal & Business Results Coach and Business Trainer

Beyond Chaos is a heroic story of a woman who has taken life by the horns and despite many great obstacles and heartbreak, has lived in a way that inspires and motivates us. Within this book are lessons from which we can all learn to make the most of this precious life. I am already hoping for a sequel!

— Karen Lanka Hedman
Entrepreneur and Wellness Coach

BEYOND CHAOS

Journey
to
Freedom and Joy

Debra Valentina

Write Path
PUBLISHING

Kapaa, Kauai, Hawaii 96746
www.WritePath.net

Beyond Chaos

Copyright ©2020 by Debra Valentina

Write Path Publishing
Kapaa, Kauai, Hawaii 96746
info@writepath.net
www.writepath.net

Cover painting: Watercolor by Debra Valentina
Cover Design: Debbie Stratton, Design Dog Studio
Interior Layout: Fusion Creative Works
Editor: Pamela Aole'a Varma

Paperback ISBN: 978-0-9970022-4-9
eBook ISBN: 978-0-9970022-5-6
Library of Congress Control Number: 2020930086

Printed in the United States of America

To my extraordinary therapists,
healers and guides (seen and unseen)
along my journey to freedom and joy

Contents

Acknowledgements

I acknowledge my maternal grandmother for cultivating my senses of curiosity, adventure and humor, and most recently for confirming the truth of my experience.

Mahalo nui loa (thank you very much) to my dear friends Rita and Patrick for their unconditional love, wisdom and modeling the path to *truly* trust Spirit.

I would like to shower love and praise upon my bestie Pam for her precious friendship, guidance, outstanding editing skills, commitment to excellence and for mirroring the truth of me.

Introduction

This book is *not* a tale of suffering, woe and victimhood, but a story of resilience, freedom and joy. I am a happy, healthy, vital woman who is up to big things.

This *is* a story of forgiveness, victory and no regret. This *is* a story of the triumph of the human spirit, trust and faith in action.

This book will take you on a journey . . . my journey. It has not always been a "bed of roses," however, I am inspired to tell you my story. I would not be the person I am today unless I had become masterful at forgiveness and trust.

I have always had a strong connection to my Higher Self, what I call my Knowingness. I believe that my Knowingness is directly connected to Spirit, Guidance, the Universe, God, Goddess, All That Is, whatever you desire to call it. I find it has been the one constant in my life and I am very grateful for my connection.

I was inspired to present my story not in chronological order, but rather grouped by the learning experiences and pivotal moments I have had. I have changed almost all the names and places in my story in order to protect the identity of those I have written about.

Allow me to take you on my journey to a free and joyful life. May you find the path to your own freedom.

Debra Valentina
February 2020

Chapter One: Hospitals and Healing

Hospital Trauma

I am *so* insulted. My emotions are boiling over. I am crying so hard I can hardly catch my breath.

"Someone please help me!"

Why am I in this crib? What is going on here in this room full of cribs?

I am a very aware three-year-old and am indignant about being in this crib because I feel like a young adult. I can walk and talk (a lot), and I am almost old enough to be in school.

I am in the pediatric ward in my New England city hospital. I am not the only one screaming, there are many screaming toddlers. How did I get here?

I have some pain in the area where I go "pee pee." In fact, it hurts so badly when I go to the bathroom that I try not to go too often.

I miss being home because this place does not feel good. I do not know anyone here.

No! I do not want to stay here. If I were in charge of this awful place, I would run it much better and would not have little people, like me, in cribs!

≈ ≈ ≈

After I was discharged from the hospital, I rode home in the back seat of my neighbor's car. I talked non-stop because I was so happy to see two people I knew, my neighbor and my mother. I had experienced so much loneliness in that hospital for those few days. My neighbor was driving because my mother didn't have a driver's license and, as usual, my father was working long hours.

That very jarring and disturbing experience in the hospital affected my career decisions. Seventeen years later, when I was a sophomore in college, I decided to become a hospital administrator in order to follow through on my desire to "do it better."

So, I earned an undergraduate degree in business, with a major in management, at the University of Massachusetts (UMass), Amherst. After a two-year healthcare internship at the UMass Health Center, I received a full traineeship and scholarship to the University of California, Berkeley and earned my master's degree in Corporate Healthcare Management.

My Protective Mind

When I was in my mid-30s, I wanted to have my horoscope read. The astrologer said I needed to know the exact time of my birth. I went to the city hospital where I was born, and where I had been in the crib as a toddler.

Not only did I find the time of my birth (9:20 am on December 31, 1953), I also learned that at age 3 I'd had a urinary tract infection (UTI) and the doctors performed tests to make sure that the infection had not affected my kidneys.

I remember my internist gasping and turning pale when I spoke with him about this early diagnosis. His reaction prompted me to do some research. I discovered, at that young age, the probability is very high that sexual abuse is the cause of the infection.

My life has been a journey of "recovery" from the trauma and drama of this abuse, which my Knowingness (what I call my Higher Self) tells me began when I was 2 years old and continued until I left for college. I did not consciously remember this abuse until I was in my mid-30s.

Minds are beautiful things. They protect you by allowing you to forget things that are horrific, that you can't handle when they occur, hiding them in dark recesses until you have the capacity to process them.

No More Santa Claus

A few days before my fifth birthday, my family and I were living in a small duplex home. It was Christmas Eve. My sisters and I were required to go to bed early so we could get up on Christmas morning to see what Santa had brought us. With all the excitement, I couldn't fall asleep.

As I lay awake with my eyes and ears open, I heard my parents arguing quite loudly. I could hear them bickering about money and that they could not afford the presents they had already bought. As usual, my father was blaming and cursing my mother.

As all of this information began to compute in my brain, I realized that what they were saying is that *they were Santa Claus* and that they weren't able to afford presents for us kids.

My first thought was, *"Oh my God, no Santa Claus!"*

My second thought was that I had suspected that Santa Claus was fake all along. It didn't really make sense to me that Santa Claus could go down chimneys and visit all those houses all over the world in one night, and I was all about making things make sense. So, at 5 years old, the illusion of Santa Claus was shattered for me, and along with it all other fairy tales.

After I got over the shock of no Santa Claus, I decided I would not allow money to stop me from doing the things I wanted to do in life. And that has been true, even when I have spent money ahead of earning it.

Are You Worth Fifty Cents or a Quarter?

One summer when I was in grade school, I wanted to buy my mother a birthday present. Even though the four of us girls had chores to do, with an allowance promised in return, we only sporadically saw the financial reward.

As my mother's birthday approached, it had been quite some time since we had received our allowance, so I had no money to buy my mother a gift. I bravely went to my father to ask for some money to surprise my mother with a present.

My father's response was to interrogate me, for what seemed a *very* long time. He put out a fifty-cent piece and a quarter and asked me to choose which one I was "worth" and then to defend my choice.

It was one of the most confusing moments of my life. Even at my young age, it felt very unfair that I would be asked to defend my worth. I had watched my friends' fathers love and support them no matter what. Wasn't my father's job to totally love me without asking me to defend my worth?

I chose the fifty-cent piece and told him what I did to deserve it: making my bed every morning, helping in the kitchen, washing the dishes, working hard to get good grades, and everything and anything I could think of. After the interrogation, my father gave me both coins.

It didn't feel like a victory because I was so stunned and mortified that I had to "prove my worth" to my own father.

Now that I've done so much internal work, I know that one's worth has little to do with what one does and much more to do with who they are being in the world. I wish I had known that when I was a little girl defending her existence to her mentally unhealthy father.

Early Influential Men

When I was a senior in college, I created an administrative residency for myself in New York City, meaning that I talked one of my professors into giving me a full semester of credits for gaining real life experience in a hospital.

Although there were some great parts to this residency, like living in Brooklyn Heights and being able to attend Broadway plays in Manhattan on the weekends, the experience involved some drama.

My "mentor" Ricardo began flirting with me and I didn't know how to handle it. I became very weepy and depressed. I thought I was doing "something wrong" for him to give me that kind of attention.

By the time I came back from New York, all I seemed to do was cry. When I went back to UMass, Amherst for my last college semester, I saw a psychologist at the health center to figure out why I was crying.

Rather than give me pills, this psychologist's solution was to introduce me to Michael, the Chief Executive Officer (CEO) of the health center. The psychologist thought I just needed to have a better experience than the one I had had in New York. I am truly grateful to this intuitive professional who did not prescribe medicine, just practical guidance.

Michael offered me a volunteer position as his administrative intern for my last college semester. I thrived as his intern, learning a lot about being a thoughtful and strong leader. Michael allowed me to "shadow" him and go to many important meetings to learn about the subtleties of leadership and making balanced decisions.

When I graduated from college, Michael offered me a paid internship and I gladly accepted. In less than a year, I was responsible for several departments. I was part of the leadership team and loved every moment of my job.

I had a huge crush on Michael. I didn't do anything about it then, but a few years later, by the time I went back to New England to work for a large health plan, he had changed jobs and was running a much larger healthcare organization in Chicago. I got in touch with Michael and told him I was thinking about coming to Chicago.

Michael invited me to stay with him and I had one of the best and most romantic weeks of my life! He was divorced and in a relationship with one of the women who still worked at the university health center, but for some reason that didn't seem to bother me. I just wanted to live out my fantasy.

That memorable week, we played tourists during the day, ate at fabulous restaurants in the evening, and made love all night. All this love and attention made me very happy and giddy.

I saw Michael several more times after that: once in Washington, DC and once in my Connecticut home for romantic "sleepovers."

The next few times after that, I saw Michael for lunch or dinner, usually while attending healthcare conferences. At our final lunch at a Chicago restaurant, I gave him a big hug goodbye and that was it. Fantasy complete.

My Vagina Talks

When I was in my early 30s, I was an executive for a large health maintenance organization (HMO) in Connecticut. I had been having sessions with a psychiatrist named Dr. G who always asked me about my dreams. I told him the ones I remembered, all pointing symbolically to the story of my sexual abuse by my father.

The dreams were about a young boy and since I was a girl, I was able to dismiss the fact that these dreams were about me. I didn't realize the boy in the dreams was a portrayal of the masculine energy I masked myself with for much of my life.

About that same time, when I felt safe enough in the presence of my about-to-be second husband, my mind allowed those years of abuse to come clearly into focus.

I was doing some energy healing work when my vagina literally began telling its story. I heard the words in my head, then I hesitantly began speaking them out loud. I was in the presence of a male healer who skillfully followed my body's lead and asked my vagina gentle question after gentle question, until the full story was revealed to both of us. I am eternally grateful to this healer for his skill in knowing how to handle this situation as it spontaneously came up.

After this healing session, pieces of my life puzzle began falling into place. For instance, it now made sense to me why I had been so afraid of men, why I had chronic UTIs and why I didn't like to go to bed early for fear someone would sneak into my room at night.

My Three Sisters

What I know, and has been confirmed by my Guidance, is that I was not the only one of my father's four daughters who was sexually abused. However, my sisters, to this day, think I am "nuts" and that I was never sexually abused. Each of them has taken on the deep denial syndrome that my generational lineage had taken on before them. That is their choice.

All three of my sisters became educators. My two older sisters were teachers in the public school system until they retired. My younger sister developed a teaching curriculum for an outpatient mental health center for children, where more than 80 percent of the children they helped had been sexually abused. She did that work for at least 25 years. I believe that was no accident.

After more than 40 years of completing various types of therapy, participating in gazillions of self-help courses, and reading hundreds of personal development books, I realize that for my sisters to admit that they had been victims of abuse would be to shatter their whole world, and they are not yet ready or willing to do that.

Chapter Two: My Family of Origin

Inducing Labor

I was told this story many times as a child, and knowing my father's personality, I believe it's true.

I was still in my mother's womb on December 30, 1953. My father was clear he wanted to get the baby out of my mother's belly and into this world so that he could take this child (me) as a tax deduction.

So, he took matters into his own hands. He took my mother on a potholed, jarring rural road, driving the car fast over the bumps, insisting on his own form of inducing labor. Well, it worked! I was born at 9:20 the following morning, just in time to be a tax deduction.

Decision: Come Into This World or Not?

Through the various forms of therapy and healing modalities I have used over the years, I have memory of being in my mother's womb. While I was growing and developing there, I was debating whether I wanted to come into this world or not.

Once I was born into my family with its high level of dysfunction, abuse, and even mental illness in the form of narcissism with my father and depression with my mother, I began wondering, "What have I done?" And yet I had chosen, so how could I ever be a victim, if I consciously chose to come into this world this lifetime?

A Curious and Lively Child

I was a very curious child. My liveliness was in direct contrast to the energy of the rest of my family. What I viscerally recall in my family's energetic and emotional dynamics is my mother being in perpetual overwhelm; my father, when he was around, always angry; and my three sisters always in blame mode, projecting the blame on me for almost everything. As I grew older, these dynamics never really changed.

There was always a lot of yelling and swearing going on between my parents. As a young girl, when this incessant screaming got to me, I would hold my breath until I turned blue and passed out. That would turn my parents' attention to me, and away from each other.

As I grew older, I would start screaming louder than my parents were yelling in order to stop the dysfunctional action. Sometimes that worked and sometimes it didn't.

When I was a young teen, my father and mother decided that I was "hyper," and my mother got a prescription from our family doctor for a drug to "calm me down." I took one pill. It made me feel weird and not myself and I never swallowed another one again. Besides, who needed the calming down? I was not the hyper one in this chaotic family.

Dysfunctional Roots

Both sets of my grandparents had dysfunctional relationships with each other and their children. My father's mother, Mariam, was nondescript, and completely under the thumb and spell of my dominating paternal grandfather. They got married when my grandmother was 18 and even when she passed away in her late 80s, she looked to me like a star-struck teenager. They had a daughter named Delia, who was my aunt.

My grandfather owned a large mixed-breed dog named Bruno, who was not particularly friendly. The dog bonded only with my grandfather and Delia, never with my grandmother Mariam.

One day Bruno bit my grandmother on the hand, sending her to the emergency room. When my grandfather came home from work that day, he was enraged at my grandmother and asked her what she had done to cause the dog to bite her, literally taking the dog's side instead of his wife's!

My Aunt Delia

Starting as a young adult, my Aunt Delia slept on the couch in the living room with her father (my grandfather). I can't remember a time when she didn't sleep there. My grandmother slept upstairs in her own bedroom.

Delia never married, never even left her father's home, and was living there when she passed on several years ago in her late 70s. Her father had died many years earlier.

My Aunt Delia was a very intelligent woman who worked at one of the local banks for well over 40 years. She walked to and from work every day until she finally got her drivers license later in life. She read a lot, mostly romance novels.

I felt very close to Delia, who was about 25 years older than me, and starting in my mid-20's, I had a strong desire to buy her gifts and take her out to do things she never would have ventured out to experience on her own. Going clothes shopping and seeing movies was such a treat for her. I felt it was a good use of my small disposable income.

In retrospect, I can totally understand why I related to my aunt so deeply. We both were being sexually abused by our fathers. When my own abuse came into clearer focus, my Guidance told me that my Aunt Delia had been abused far longer than I had, since she had never left her father's home. And as I started to reflect on her sleeping arrangement, along with other clues like my grandfather calling her "Babe" and her always riding in the front seat of the car with my grandfather, while my grandmother was relegated to the back seat, it made sense to me.

I felt strongly that I wanted to bring a little joy into Delia's life. When I moved away from my hometown, I continued to connect with her by calling her to share my life's adventures and by sending her postcards whenever I traveled to a new place.

Generational Pattern . . . Both Sides of the Family

I experienced sexual inappropriateness by men on both sides of my family.

My mother's father, Ronald, was an alcoholic. Being a family of deep denial, no one talked about his addiction. Grandpa Ronald was also a bit nondescript, not unlike my father's mother.

Two incidents stand out in my mind when I think about him.

One summer when I was about 7 years old, my mother, sisters and I visited Pennsylvania for our usual two-week stay with our grandparents. One day my grandfather took me to do errands with him. For our last stop, he took me to the local bar in the middle of the afternoon. While my grandfather had his beer, he ordered a Shirley Temple for me. I was thrilled with the adventure, although I did wonder what we were doing in a bar in the middle of the afternoon.

When I was a young teen, we paid another summer visit to our grandparents. I was happy to see my Grandpa Ronald. We hugged for a long time. The next thing I knew he put his hand on my left breast for a few seconds, long enough for me to know that it indeed happened. I was shocked, very disappointed, and didn't tell a soul. However, I didn't repress the memory of this incident, as I had done with the sexual abuse and incest by my father, probably because I was older and more fully aware that his behavior was egregious.

My Knowingness confirms that the sexual abuse was a generational pattern in my family going back many generations. When I left home at age 18 to go to college, I began my earnest healing journey to become whole, and I participated in some powerful generational therapy.

My Beloved Grandmother Elaine

My mother's mother Elaine was a strong, bright, tenacious woman who had great intuition. I believe she suspected my father's abusive nature. Grandma Elaine is the only family member I really respected. She was the only one who "got me," and I feel her presence from the other side urging me to write this book.

One of the things I loved most about Grandma Elaine was that she was able to laugh at herself. She had a fabulous sense of humor and thought life was funny. I happily adopted this, and it is a belief that has served me well. My own sense of humor and perspective during my life's downs was, and still is, very helpful.

Love Affair with Kauai

After my junior year in high school, my beloved Grandma Elaine gifted my mother, younger sister and me an organized tour of the four major Hawaiian Islands: Oahu, Hawaii (the Big Island), Maui and Kauai.

When Grandma was in her late 60s and early 70s, she worked for several years in a school cafeteria, with the sole purpose of earning enough money to take us on this trip. She had taken my two older sisters on special trips, and wanted to make sure she treated all her grandchildren equally. In her mind she "owed" us this trip.

Kauai was, by far, my favorite island. I have a vivid memory of our last stop before we left the island. The tour guide took us to a *heiau*, a Hawaiian place of worship, at a place named Lydgate Park. I spent some quiet time in this sacred place, used by ancient Hawaiians as a place of refuge. Being there felt so soothing, grounding and safe. I remember sobbing because "I didn't want to leave home."

I never forgot this feeling, and over the years went back to Kauai many times.

Chapter Three: Chaos and Jealousy

Hoover Vacuum

At a very young age I was aware that my family wasn't handling life well. One of my coping strategies was to be helpful. I have a memory at age 5 when I decided I would clean the house since no one seemed to be taking care of our home. I took out the heavy Hoover vacuum cleaner, that was taller than me, and began vacuuming the house. I realize, in retrospect, that it was not only helping my family, but it was helping me feel more in control of what seemed like constant upheaval in our home.

Classmate Jealousy

One of my most traumatic school events happened when I was in Miss Jones' sixth grade class. At the beginning of the school year, Miss Jones announced that she believed that "no one was perfect." Therefore, she declared, "No student will be getting straight As in my class." Well, being the driven perfectionist that I had become by then, I earned all As, and Miss Jones gave them to me on my report card.

I shared these report card results with another girl in my class when she asked me. I was all about telling the truth, since that was not happening in my family.

Well, this girl shared my report card results with the entire class. It gave some of the other smart kids in the class an opportunity to bully me. I received phone calls at home, and even at my paternal grandparents' home on weekends, harassing me about "how smart I was" in mocking tones. I was so upset. It felt relentless.

What was even worse was that I was embarrassed to tell my parents, and I did not trust them to help me, as they had no history of assisting me, so I kept this burden all to myself. I was looking forward to getting to seventh grade to finally put it behind me.

Hellish Embarrassment

Within a few short months after seventh grade began, I inadvertently expelled gas in front of three of the "smart boys" in my class, and they harassed me for most of the year. Whenever I was near them, they made mimicking noises of expelling gas, reminding me of the original incident. Of course, as was my pattern, I did not tell anyone that this was occurring as I thought it was my fault and that I had done something wrong.

A gaseous stomach was a frequent occurrence for me well into my 30s. This symptom was finally diagnosed as Irritable Bowel Syndrome (IBS) by my doctor, the same internist who gasped at the UTI diagnosis I received as a toddler. I am very grateful that as I have healed emotionally over the years, my IBS has healed as well.

How I managed to get through seventh grade without some sort of breakdown seems amazing to me. While all this bullying was going on, I continued to excel at my schoolwork and spelling. I loved to spell and participated in citywide spelling bees. I was often among the top winners. As I look back at my younger self, I am awed by her resilience and ability to excel during this incessant harassment by three boys.

As an introspective adult, I now see how these bullying incidents were related to how my sisters treated me. The three boys who bullied me were in both my sixth and seventh grade classes. They were jealous I had received all As from Miss Jones. My sisters were jealous and picked on me because they thought that I received more attention from my father than they did.

Yes, I got attention from my father, but sexual molestation was not the type of attention I deserved. I craved encouragement and acknowledgement.

Telling My Truth and Forgiveness

When I was in my mid-50s, I decided I would no longer buy into the family secret about abuse, and so I wrote and sent a brief, clear letter to my father describing my truth. I knew that the relationship with him, my mother and my siblings would no longer be the same. However, I needed to take this big leap to keep my sanity, for living a lie was becoming much more painful than telling the truth.

The day I went to the post office to send the letter, I sent it registered, requiring my father's signature, so I would know when he received it. As I anticipated, this letter led to a string of events that culminated in no longer being in communication with my parents (who have now passed) and my sisters. Some may call this being "estranged" from my family. I view it as a conscious choice to take care of myself. Being blamed and judged for someone else's harmful actions was not loving myself.

Interestingly, I feel freer from choosing not to engage with my family than any other action I have taken in my life. I live with the fact that most people believe that one should be in touch with family no matter what. This is not my truth. I am so happy I chose freedom over other people's opinions about what is right for my life.

As I said, my parents have passed on, and both have communicated with me from the "other side." Both my father and my mother have asked me for forgiveness for how each behaved as a parent. I have forgiven them both. I have also forgiven my three living sisters.

Chapter Four: Young Leadership

My First Best Friend

When I was in the first grade, our family moved to Elm Street, a middle-class neighborhood in the same New England city where we'd been living. My new teacher said I was behind because my new school was further ahead in the curriculum than my old school.

I was horrified to be behind on anything, and spent sleepless nights trying to figure out how to catch up. My 6-year-old self feverishly worked to catch up so I would no longer be behind. In my short life, I had picked up the notion that I needed to be perfect, perhaps so that the craziness in my family would stop and so I would finally be acknowledged for something, anything.

The one good thing that happened in this new school is that I found my first best friend, an only child named Caroline. Her parents had been looking for someone to be Caroline's surrogate sister. I felt very fortunate.

I loved being with Caroline and her mother, and there were some beautiful perks to being Caroline's "sister." When Caroline's mother bought her presents, and if I were with Caroline that day, I would get a present too! The three of us did all kinds of fun things after school and on weekends. I especially loved shopping for clothes. Dressing fashionably and artistically became part of my identity, and is a part of my identity today.

I also got to go on trips with Caroline and her family. I fondly remember a long weekend to New Jersey. I remember not only the happy anticipation of the mini vacation, but also the excitement of taking a day off from school. When we got to New Jersey, Caroline and I had a wonderful time, especially playing by and in the Atlantic Ocean. I felt so lighthearted and carefree.

When I feel carefree, my innate sense of humor comes out, as it did that weekend. Caroline's father noticed, and commented on how funny I was. I was so proud. To get a huge compliment like that from Caroline's father was a big deal for me. My father never complimented me on anything. No matter what I did, it was never enough: earning straight As, cleaning the house with a large vacuum. Nothing, and I mean nothing was good enough.

Candy Striper

At age 12, I intentionally volunteered as a candy striper at the local hospital in the very same pediatric ward I had been in when I was 3 years old – *in the very same room*. I was a great candy striper as I listened and paid a great deal of attention to the children who were confined in this room with so many other sick children. I was giving them the attention I craved and had not received so many years before.

I worked as a candy striper for four years. When I turned 16, I was asked by the volunteer coordinator to apply for a paying job at the hospital.

Productivity and Young Leadership

As a high school student, I worked in both the hospital cafeteria and kitchen. It was very physical work. I developed large muscles in my arms from carrying so many hospital trays to the patients. It felt satisfying and freeing being productive and making money for the first time. I was thrilled to afford new clothes with the money I earned.

My father was a member of the Masons, a very old religious organization with high moral standards. He was adamant that his four daughters be in the Rainbow Girls, an organization for the daughters of Masons. My father was also a lay minister at our Protestant church, meaning he was allowed to preach sermons from the pulpit. It seems so ironic to me that my father could be a "pillar of the community," yet be so abusive in his private life.

Despite my cognitive dissonance about my father's participation in the Masons, I am grateful for the leadership training I received as a young woman from being involved in the Rainbow Girls. When I became the leader, or Worthy Advisor, of our local group, I was responsible for being a model to the other young women, conducting the meetings and raising money to keep the organization financially sound. I continued on to a role in the national Rainbow Girls.

In addition to the huge time commitment to the Rainbow Girls, I was among the top of my class, worked at the hospital, tutored students in math and reading, played flute in both the school orchestra and marching band, volunteered on various projects and participated in several social clubs. It was quite the juggling act.

When I look back on this now, I see a driven young woman who did a lot, and to my amazement, very well. Yet, despite these accomplishments, I still felt empty inside and felt as if I needed to do more to fill that void.

Not In the "In-Crowd"

In high school, I was in the "smart kids" class and we were labeled the "dorks." My high school placed all the intelligent kids in the same class, so from 10th through 12th grade, I was in every class with the same 25-plus teens. I played the flute in the marching band, which was considered the epitome of being a dork.

Even though I was not part of the in-crowd, I wished to be. However, I can now see the benefits of how I played it. I was good friends with several girls, but none of them were friends with each other. This gave me an opportunity to be friends with a variety of people and not feel as much peer pressure.

I was never really interested in what the in-crowd was doing anyway. No drinking, no drugs for this girl. In the pursuit to be perfect, I was in the "goodie two shoes" category. Instead of drinking alcohol on weekends, I attended the theater with Caroline and her mother.

Caroline's mother was on a mission to have her daughter be "cultured" and one of the ways to do this, she thought, was to expose her to the theater, and thankfully, I got to go along. To this day, I love the theater.

A powerful benefit to not being in the "in crowd" is that I learned to think my own thoughts and make my own choices. I don't follow trends or others and that has served me very well throughout my life.

Chapter Five: Path to Feeling Worthy

My Father's Son

My father desperately wanted a son, which he never got. I took that to heart and became that son, to the point of acting like a man, especially during my corporate experience in my 20s and early 30s, with the hope of him expressing love for me.

After graduating from the University of California Berkeley, I worked for one of the largest managed care companies in the country, which had a strict dress code. When I look back at myself in those days, it's jarring. My "uniform" was a navy-blue boxed suit, closed-toed navy shoes to match, with my long hair tied back, so it would appear as if I had short hair. I had so much male energy running through my body, I even looked masculine to myself.

I was competent, productive and rewarded well for exuding masculine energy. I made my way up the company's corporate ladder in record time to become the youngest chief operating officer (COO) in the system, which involved transferring to Connecticut. Becoming a COO had been a long-term goal of mine, tracing back to my 3-year-old self in the hospital ward.

I thought I would be ecstatic when I achieved this goal. But instead of being ecstatic, I was miserable.

I was angry and upset, and I began to project these feelings onto others. One day I started yelling over the phone at an art vendor who had not delivered what I had expected.

After I hung up, I realized something was terribly wrong. That is not how I normally acted, I never yelled. *What was going on? Why was I so angry?*

As I began to examine the situation, I realized that even though I had attained my childhood dream, I was not happy. I needed to look at this more closely.

Dr. G

I asked my friend, the mental health director of the health center, in confidence, if she could refer me to a therapist, and that is how I ended up seeing Dr. G, the psychiatrist and medical director of a highly respected mental health institution in Connecticut. Although he no longer saw patients due to his administrative duties, he was willing to see me as a favor to my friend.

This began my more serious introspection to get to the bottom of my unhappiness. At the end of my first couple of sessions with Dr. G, he said he thought that it would be beneficial for me to see him three times a week for a while. *Three times a week?* It really shook me up to think I would be seeing a psychiatrist that often, but I was very committed to heal and to turn my life into a joyful experience.

For a handful of months, I did visit Dr. G three times a week, and to my relief, I began to feel better. I answered his questions and shared my dreams. Being able to share my feelings and have someone listen, receive and truly understand me was a totally new experience.

To this day, I am grateful to Dr. G for helping me to start to unwind my complex history and to begin my real healing.

Negotiating My Exit

About two years into my tenure as COO of this health plan, my boss, the chief executive officer (CEO) of the region, spent six months at the Wharton Executive Program. While she was away, her replacement was the CEO from another region. He was not like my nurturing boss Karen. He was hands-off, and more interested in flirting with the female sales team than assisting me.

An issue that a colleague of mine brought to Karen's attention, while she was away, was the long wait line in the pharmacy. (The pharmacy was one of my departmental responsibilities.) I did not address the issue quickly enough, so Karen called the interim CEO and told him to "get it fixed."

Even though I had "walked on water" a few months earlier with an excellent performance review and a healthy salary increase, the interim CEO and Karen decided that I was now incompetent, which was not the case as I saw it.

As I look back with more perspective, what I see now is two things at play. The first is that because I wanted to be perfect, I had a hard time asking for assistance in a timely manner. Secondly, the CEO had a need to blame me instead of help me. Once again, the pattern of being blamed showed up in my life.

By the time Karen returned from Wharton, I was ready to leave my position as soon as I found a new one. I negotiated the time to look for a new job, as well as to receive the vested money the company had matched in my retirement fund.

I felt good about negotiating on my own behalf and I exited with my integrity intact. I was in my early 30s.

Move to Pittsburgh

Before I left the Connecticut health plan, I was hired to be the CEO of another plan based in Pittsburgh and moved there not knowing anyone. I moved into a hotel until my temporary apartment was available.

Within a few days of being in Pittsburgh, I attended a seminar on excellence during which I got up and shared in front of about 100 or so people that I had just moved to Pittsburgh. With microphone in hand, I announced that I didn't know anyone in Pittsburgh and I suddenly began sobbing. How embarrassing!

After the seminar, a line of people quickly formed in front of me, each person offering to be my friend. As it turns out, many of those who declared their willingness to be my friend did become my friend, one of whom became my second husband, Gupta.

My CEO job in Pittsburgh lasted about a year. The company that hired me was bought by a much larger insurance company and this new company had a plan to replace the old company's CEOs within a short period of time.

As I got wind of this replacement plan, I decided that I would negotiate my exit before I was asked to leave. I negotiated a lump sum portion of my salary, which I was able to use to start my own healthcare consulting and coaching practice.

This was the second time that I had negotiated with a Goliath organization. I am proud of myself for being proactive and negotiating well on my own behalf.

Chapter Six: Sex, Money and Men

Business Partners with a Sex Addict

Soon after I started my consulting practice, I got a call from a woman I thought was a friend, asking me if I would be willing to talk to her husband David, an architect, about the possibility of going into business with him. I was open to meeting with the two of them.

I was intrigued with the possibility of creating functional health-care spaces, which I had the opportunity to do many times during my seven-year tenure at the large managed care company.

For a short time, David and I did go into business together marketing the design of beautiful healthcare spaces.

A few months into our business partnership, David began kissing me on the lips to say hello in the morning. I felt very uncomfortable and knew something was off. I ended the business relationship quickly and moved on.

As it turned out, David was a sex addict, which his wife knew and did not tell me. She told another friend of ours, who felt it was important to share that information with me. Since my father was a sex addict as well, at first it had felt oddly comfortable to be with him. I am glad I extracted myself from that situation promptly.

Early Years with Gupta

After that first night in Pittsburgh at the excellence seminar, I kept running into Gupta at other seminars. We had some of the same friends and ended up at parties together. We became friends, then dated.

One of the things that attracted me the most to Gupta was his thirst to become "enlightened" in this lifetime. He was an avid "seeker" and sought out all the latest and greatest spiritual courses. I followed his lead and enrolled in most of the courses that he did. We became spiritual co-adventurers.

I wanted to marry Gupta, but he was hesitant, so I requested that we go to couples' therapy with a mutual therapist friend of ours. After his considerations were worked out in our sessions, he was finally ready to take the leap.

As I look back on it, I am not quite sure why I was so anxious to marry him. I liked Gupta's spiritual curiosity, as well as his intellectual and emotional support as I maneuvered through the first few years of my own business, but we rarely had sex and that was OK with me. As my abuse history became clearer, it made more sense to me that sex was not one of my priorities.

Sexless Marriage

Gupta and I got married. Over time, our occasional sex turned into no lovemaking for nearly 15 years. As I healed, the lack of sex became an issue for me. Also, as the years progressed, I had become less masculine and much more feminine in my nature.

Gupta always had a lot of feminine energy and when I became more comfortable in expressing my feminine essence, there was no polarity between the two of us. Neither one of us had a desire to initiate sex.

It is amazing to me that it took so many years to notice that I wasn't really satisfied with not having sex. We had intimate conversations, but that is just not the same as physical intimacy.

White Woman in India

Gupta was born in Calcutta. We visited India together periodically and even lived there for a few months while Gupta had work in his home country.

Whenever I traveled to India, my natural curiosity helped me cope with the many differences between India and the United States. I also made a commitment to myself that no matter what occurred, I would not complain. This commitment was not always easy to keep, but for the most part I lived up to it.

There's no comparison to living in a developing country like India with being in a developed nation like the U.S. I am proud of myself for being able to acculturate well while in India for an extended period, especially in a place where women are largely treated as less than equal to men.

On one visit to India, Gupta and I arrived in Mumbai (on our way to Calcutta) at 3 a.m. By the time we got our luggage and cleared Customs it was even later. Gupta's relatives went to get the driver who was waiting in a long line amidst thousands and thousands of people greeting arriving travelers.

While Gupta and I were trying to reunite with his relatives, I lost him. In an instant, I was surrounded by Indian beggars who were getting closer and closer, and more aggressive, by the second.

I called in my Guardian Angels and starting yelling Gupta's name. I could hear him, but with the vast number of people outside the airport, I couldn't see him. My heart was beating fast, but I knew that I was protected by Spirit and would not be touched or harmed.

After what seemed like hours (it was only minutes), Gupta found me and whisked me off to the waiting car with a driver. Having a driver was in direct contrast to the prevalence of beggars I had just been surrounded by.

And India is chock full of contrasts.

Most of Gupta's relatives would be considered wealthy, with several servants and cooks living in their homes. Gupta's mother also had servants, though he, or rather, I, was supporting her lifestyle, as I'll detail in a later chapter.

It was always a bit disconcerting to go outside his mother's home in Calcutta to witness more than a million, at that time, people living on the streets. They were not labeled homeless. The streets *were* their home.

The lack of infrastructure in India continually surprised me. For example, no matter how well-off Gupta's relatives were, when the electricity went out, as it did quite often, there was never a back-up plan. I vividly remember one very hot summer in New Delhi, where a few of Gupta's aunts live, sleeping outdoors when the electricity and air conditioning went out.

Subjugation of Indian Women

One thing I never got used to, and is not OK with me, is how women are treated in India. I was last in India over 15 years ago, and while I had hoped conditions for women would improve, I understand that by and large, they are still similar in certain areas of the country.

Two of Gupta's aunts, his mother's sisters, whom I got to know well, were highly educated, yet were subjugated by their husbands. One was a physician and was treated very poorly. Her husband talked to her in an extremely condescending manner and yelled at her often while I was visiting their home. It was just considered "the way it was."

I still feel angered when I replay in my mind the scenes I watched of women being treated dramatically less than equals.

One time I was traveling on a long overnight train trip across northern India, from New Delhi to Mumbai, with Gupta's mother, sister and nephew. His mother insisted that I go in first class while they traveled in the back of the train.

In first class we were served a multi-course meal. I learned the pecking order on that trip by the order in which the Indian family sharing the first-class car with me, and I, were served: Indian husband, white woman (me), Indian son, then Indian wife. I was shocked and asked the wife to eat with me several times, but she didn't budge.

In some areas of India, women still need to dress "decently," i.e. no showing of their upper arms, even in the height of a sweltering summer. Indian men can wear whatever they want.

One very hot summer, I vividly remember fantasizing not only of wearing a sleeveless dress or blouse, but just going stark naked, but instead reluctantly followed the Indian custom of "covering up," for the sake of keeping the peace with Gupta's mother and relatives.

In India, it is acceptable for men to get divorced, but not for women. One of Gupta's female cousins got divorced and she was shunned by the community and most of the relatives. She was very independent and after her divorce, found a boyfriend. I recognized that this rebellious behavior was unusual for an Indian woman.

The treatment I am describing is in the middle to upper classes of India. I understand that there is even more of an inequality gap between men and women in the rural areas where most women are child brides and intentionally kept illiterate and uneducated.

This in-your-face inequality was very challenging for me to endure while in India. But rather than be discouraged, I gained even more resolve to be treated equally to men.

Traveling Northern India with My Mother-in-Law

In 1993, after I completed an exhausting nationwide project of recruiting physicians and mental health providers for a Preferred Provider Organization (PPO) in the United States, I decided to take a break. At the same time, Gupta secured a consulting gig in southeast India near Vizag and I decided to go with him.

We flew to Calcutta, where Gupta visited with his mom for a few days before he flew south to work. I traveled in northern India with his mother, sister and nephew before reuniting with him in the south.

The few weeks traveling with Gupta's relatives were very rich. We first visited New Delhi, then had a driver take us north to the "hill station" of Mussoorie (a misnomer as far as I am concerned since it is over 6,000 feet in elevation).

In Mussoorie, Gupta's aunt Manisha and uncle had a beautiful home overlooking a bluff that had a 180-degree view of the mountains. It was a steep slope to get down to their home. Upon my arrival, I sat on an outside bench to rest and Manisha sat next to me. I heard myself utter the words "I'm home." And she said, "Yes, I know. Welcome home." Little did I know more was to be revealed.

Past Life Memories in Mussoorie

A few days later, Gupta's uncle was playing bridge at a buddy's home a mile or so away. Manisha and I joined them a bit later for high tea, my favorite "meal" of the day in India. After tea, Manisha and I decided to walk home, since the bridge game was taking longer than expected.

Well, it turned out Manisha did not know the way. When we found ourselves on a road that was not taking us back home, I had a vague recognition. I knew this road.

Then I saw a black wrought iron fence that was grown over with thick weeds. I had a remembrance of this place. I had a vision and deep feeling of being a happy nun in the once-thriving orchard where I picked peaches when they were in season.

I asked Manisha what this place had been. She said it used to be a nunnery with a lovely peach orchard. Oh my God, I was having a very vivid and accurate past life memory! Manisha had similar memories. We had been nuns together in this very place.

"Madame": Being Queen in South India

Several weeks later, I flew to Vizag where Gupta was staying in a plush hotel while he was doing his consulting gig in a rural town many miles outside Vizag. Each morning his driver picked him up from the hotel, along with a couple of other consultants, and I would have the whole day to myself. It was one of the most relaxing times of my life.

Most days I was the only guest in the hotel, and I was treated like a queen, which I thoroughly enjoyed. The kitchen staff had notes regarding what "Madame's" breakfast and my other dietary preferences were.

My days consisted of getting out of bed late, being served my preferred breakfast in my room, watching funny English TV soap operas, going to the pool to swim and read, walking around the grounds, and going to the bar for a cold soda (tasted so good in the heat) to wait for Gupta to arrive "home" from his day. We then would have a gourmet Indian meal made to order with our picky preferences (not as many hot spices as South Indians prefer). This exquisite pampering lasted for many weeks.

After a few months living in India, Gupta's project was complete, and it was time to go home to the United States. Although I was happy to be returning to what was familiar and to create my next entrepreneurial projects, I was sad to leave my relaxed days and the luxury of being "Queen."

"I Was the Best Dad"

While Gupta and I were living in Scottsdale, Arizona, my parents came to visit. One evening, the four of us were eating a delicious Indian meal I had painstakingly prepared. During dinner, seemingly out of nowhere, my father declared, "I was the best dad any daughter could have wished for. Isn't that right, Debbie?" (My family still called me Debbie which I hated because it made me feel little and powerless, like I did as a child).

I was shocked and decided to remove some dishes from the dining table into the kitchen so that I would not have to respond. Gupta came into the kitchen and whispered to me, "I know that's not true, but just agree with him, so that we can keep the peace."

What? Are you frickin' kidding me?

There is no way in hell I was going to say that my father was the best dad ever, after enduring at least 16 years of sexual and emotional abuse.

While we were in the kitchen, my father proceeded to get louder with his proclamations of being an outstanding dad. Still I didn't respond. Finally, my father began to chuckle with a haunting undertone. I stayed in the kitchen making up things to do so I would not have to return to the table.

Although I knew his words were consistent with how he had always seen himself as a parent, I felt outraged and incredulous that my father could be so out of touch with reality. I could hardly wait until my parents left, knowing I would never invite them to my home again.

After the incident finally passed, as was the family pattern, my parents, Gupta and I acted as if nothing happened. A pattern of total denial for all "bad things" that happened within the family.

The worst thing about this whole scenario is that I felt hugely betrayed by Gupta. He knew every detail of the abuse that I could remember (to this day I can't remember all the details and I am grateful for this fact). Gupta's priority to "keep the peace" trumped backing up his wife. It took me quite some time to forgive him for this. I was finally able to forgive Gupta when I realized that "keeping the peace" was his primary and automatic survival mechanism.

I also recognized that not forgiving him, or anyone else, was just hurting myself.

Mother's Show-stopping Moment

On this same visit to Scottsdale, my mother, Gupta and I were in our car on the way to do some errands. Gupta was driving, my mother was in the front passenger seat, and I was in the middle back seat so I could participate in the three-way conversation. Again, seemingly out of nowhere, my mother declared, "You know Debbie, I did not want you. For me, I had had enough children."

Why are you telling me this now?

Gupta was so stunned that he slowed the car down to a crawl in the middle of traffic. He turned around to me and through our eyes, we both acknowledged what my mother had just said. And then my mother proceeded by talking about something totally unimportant, like what kind of groceries we were going to buy when we got to the store. There was never any further discussion about the "bomb" that my mother exploded in the car that day.

When I think of this bizarre incident now, it seems as if my mother needed to reveal this "secret." I don't know if she felt any better after having revealed it. It felt as though she didn't remember what she said after it came out of her mouth.

I felt stunned and terribly hurt. And at the same time, I could feel this was true for my mother. I had always felt her emotion of overwhelm, and part of me could understand that having two children was already more than enough for her.

I was very grateful that I had already had many years of introspective work before this happened so at least a part of me could understand my mother's viewpoint.

Money Matters

When Gupta and I got married, both of us were employed. I was working on a project for a Chicago-based PPO developing their national network and Gupta was working as a project manager for an information technology company.

After four years of marriage, we moved to Scottsdale, and Gupta was laid off from his company about a year later. Several months after that, he got another job at a large accounting firm in the project management department, and again, this time in less than a year, he was laid off.

After that Gupta didn't really try to find a job. Seven years later, I was still the sole breadwinner in our household. During the seventh year, it became clear to me that, in fact, Gupta preferred to meditate three times a day, and if I was willing to pay the bills, he would never look for a job in earnest.

This epiphany was another "Oh my God" moment. I had not agreed to be the sole provider.

I had not signed up for this!

At the time I was seeing yet another healer/therapist. I remember mentioning I was feeling exhausted. Her response was "Ya think?" She proceeded to say, "You do realize that you not only are making the money, but you are doing *everything* in this relationship."

Sure enough, I *was* doing everything. The only things Gupta handled were paying some bills with the money I earned and doing a couple of loads of laundry.

This lopsided arrangement was not OK with me. I needed to have more of a mutual responsible partnership.

How had I not seen this? Had I gotten the deep denial gene from my family?

"You Are Not As Spiritual As I Am"

The final straw with Gupta took place when I came back from a personal development course about the power of one's beliefs.

Gupta declared, "Even though you learned a lot from this course, I am still more spiritually advanced than you."

I must not be hearing this correctly.

Gupta proceeded to express, in several different ways, that he believed I was his devotee and that he was my guru.

I was enraged.

Yes, Gupta had introduced me to some spiritual courses and practices over the years, however, introducing me to some new things did not make him my guru!

I knew I loved him, but this relationship was no longer a healthy one for me. I began to strategize on how I might leave in a graceful way.

Chapter Seven: Freedom and Feminine Essence

Entrepreneurial Freedom

I started my own healthcare consulting company in 1986. It was inevitable because, at my core, I have an entrepreneurial, independent nature and it had started to bubble over. I contracted with my first healthcare client before I left my CEO job in Pittsburgh. Having a contract before I left my job was my sign from the Universe that I was moving in the right direction.

I loved the freedom that having my own business provided me. I didn't have to be at work at a set time. I was able to work in my own natural rhythm, which meant, and still means, starting work, after my meditation and contemplation time, between 9:30 and 10:00 am and ending when I have done what I have chosen to do or need to do for that day.

After I disengaged from David the architect, I decided not to lean on anyone else, and to make this consulting company work on my own. And I did. I had, and still do have loyal clients I have fostered by creating trusting relationships with them and producing high quality results.

Managed Care Expert

Within the first several years of my business, I gained a reputation as a managed care expert. I created a niche as a negotiator of managed care contracts for hospitals and medical practices. This was such a great niche because hospitals had not yet hired an in-house managed care staff. They outsourced this responsibility and I was often contracted for these challenging negotiations.

I also became the "go to" person for the local business newspaper on managed care issues and I was contracted by the hospital association to write a white paper on managed care in western Pennsylvania. These engagements worked to my favor and I was named the "Managed Care Expert" for the *Directory of Experts* that was used widely by the media to find subject matter experts.

When Gupta and I moved to Scottsdale, I was working on three entrepreneurial ventures at the same time. I continued my healthcare consulting and coaching practice which consisted of managed care negotiations and operational projects, as well as coaching executive and entrepreneurial women from all walks of life. I also created a for-profit Women in Healthcare mentoring, educational and networking organization which grew to a membership of 350 in Phoenix, Tucson and Los Angeles.

New Business Partnership

I was co-owner of a third company, a holistic wellness program, with Alex, a psychologist. I was introduced to Alex through his wife Sally. She and Gupta became friends after they met through a self-development course. Alex had developed a very effective wellness program in the Phoenix area that helped people who frequently visited doctors without an apparent medical reason for doing so. In the startup phase, I became his partner for sweat equity and was named CEO.

One of my main responsibilities was to introduce this successful program to managed care decision makers with the goal that one would become interested in purchasing the program and our company. I was successful in getting the mental health division of one of the largest U.S. healthcare systems interested enough to sign a letter of intent to purchase the program. This was a huge victory!

And then, as often happens in the healthcare world, the mental health division was bought by a larger healthcare company and the deal was off the table. If the deal had gone through, our company would have sold for millions of dollars.

This "almost sale" was a huge disappointment. This incident curbed our motivation, and the program fizzled out until years later when Alex decided to revive it. I am so glad I chose to believe my life's journey was to go in another direction, and I continued creating new experiences for myself.

I was working particularly hard during these years, because even though Gupta was no longer employed, we had chosen to maintain the lifestyle that he and I had become accustomed to. Prior to moving to Scottsdale, I had had a lucrative consulting gig that allowed me to build a beautiful 3,500 square-foot home that required a substantial income to maintain.

After 14 years of marriage, Gupta and I divorced in 2005. After the divorce I stayed in Scottsdale for about a year and a half, but I could feel the expectation from Gupta that we would remain close friends, and that was not what I wanted.

Developing My Feminine Essence in Seattle

I decided to move to Seattle to be with my dear friend Candy on Mercer Island. I found a beautiful apartment within walking distance of Candy's home where she lived with her husband and teenage children.

I became part of the "goddess community" in the Seattle area. The women in this community had an intention to become more expressive about their feminine energy. I loved this because I was still feeling a bit of a hangover from the male energy running through my veins after being sole breadwinner for so long. It felt so natural, safe and calming, like coming home, to be part of this supportive, loving female community.

Most of us in the goddess community were participating in seminars, in both Seattle and southwestern Canada, led ironically by an East Indian man. One of the courses he created and led was very impactful for me. The exercises tapped into my feminine essence like no other self-development course had done previously.

For me, this experiential three-day course was about trusting men again. Given my history, trusting men was a courageous leap of faith. I realized it was time to stop lumping all men into the same category as my father and Gupta.

When I returned to Seattle after the class, my friends commented that I looked 10 years younger. Trusting my Guidance to attend this class really paid off!

After two-and-a-half years living in green Seattle, I decided to leave. It rains a lot there, at least nine months of the year, and that is *way* too much for me. My friend Candy had the SAD disease, Seasonal Affective Disorder, which means that she was not getting enough Vitamin D due to the lack of sun. I was very aware that the many gloomy days in Seattle made me grumpy and I didn't want to be affected by SAD.

Glorious La Jolla Beaches

I happily relocated to beautiful La Jolla in Southern California and found an apartment that was a block and a half from the beach, a dream come true! While in both Seattle and La Jolla, I continued my work as an executive and life coach and workshop facilitator, and took on fewer healthcare consulting gigs.

In between work and dating a bit, I spent a lot of time walking the beaches. As was true when I was younger, the sand and waves calmed my soul. It was my sweet escape to heaven.

Taking a Stand For Myself

In addition to coaching and facilitating personal development workshops, I became an adjunct professor of communications and healthcare administration at a national for-profit university. I went through a rigorous process to be hired, with many months of interviews and training classes to teach "their way." When I was hired, I was certified to teach more than a dozen different classes. I could have taught full-time if I had wanted to, but I wanted to balance the teaching with my other professional endeavors.

What became clear early on is that the "for-profit" status greatly influenced this university. Most of the healthcare administration students were on the GI bill and got reimbursed for the classes as long as they received a passing grade. My experience was that many of these students were not particularly inspired or engaged.

This was very disappointing to me. I had always studied hard as a student, and in college, graduate school and my post-graduate program I worked particularly hard. I was used to being in competitive schools like Berkeley and Stanford where everyone worked their butts off.

I felt as if the students acted entitled. I felt angry and confused as to why they would not want to take full advantage of this privilege they had been given of not having to pay for their education. I am so very grateful for the scholarships I received for my Berkeley education and that my Stanford post-graduate program was paid by my employer.

At this university, I was involved in an unfortunate incident. A male student in one of my classes frequently sent me negative messages online via the university portal. I felt like I was being stalked.

I reported this to my boss and administrators at the school, assuming they would assist me with handling the situation. Instead of helping me, they essentially took the student's side. I was appalled that this university would not address egregious student behavior. Intuitively I knew they wanted to continue to cater to federally reimbursed students, which this student was, due to their profit motivation.

I was outraged and promptly turned in my resignation. This definitive action was a turning point in taking a stand for myself when being harassed. This incident finally put a stop to my "being bullied" history.

Chapter Eight: **Big Loves**

George, My First Love

My first heartthrob was George Stein, from the 4th grade through high school. We were both flutists. We sat next to one another from elementary school through junior high in the all-school band. This was such a thrill for me. I got to know George well during these band rehearsals. He called himself a "renaissance man." What I loved about him most was his rebellious, independent thinking, as I related to this attitude myself.

The other time I got to see George was when I attended the local synagogue on Saturday mornings with one of my best girlfriends. This gave me the opportunity to sit behind him, and I could not have been happier. I was not Jewish, but how could I pass up an opportunity to "be with" George?

Starting in junior high, George had girlfriends, on and off. These relationships never seemed to last too long. I was in my own fantasy world that George and I would go off into the sunset together, so I never paid much attention to his girlfriends.

George was friends with the three boys who bullied me in seventh grade, but I forgave him for being a peripheral part of this. *I was so in love.* In high school, Caroline and I used to walk to his girlfriend's house (the one that lasted the longest) in hopes I would get a glimpse of him.

One Saturday night George came walking out of his girlfriend's house, and Caroline and I made up some wild (and not believable) excuse about why we were in the area and proceeded to walk him home. I was, once again, thrilled.

When I was a junior in high school, a dream of mine came true. It was Halloween night and the high school band always marched in the Halloween parade. That evening some hecklers on the sidelines were throwing eggs at the band members. I, and several others, were pelted with eggs — lots of them.

My hair turned yellow and gooey. Never one to back down, I held my head high and kept playing my flute next to George. When we arrived back at the high school, I was standing next to George and he slipped his hand into mine. *Oh my God, we were holding hands!* My fantasy about George was really happening! What I remember next is that he offered me a ride home. Of course, I said yes. In front of my house, we spent some time talking and then we began to make out. George did not have a girlfriend at the time, and I was hoping my time had come.

Then our making out turned a corner that I was not comfortable with. George tried to get to "first base" with me, i.e. touch my breast.

I knew immediately this didn't feel OK with me. At the time I didn't know why I felt so adamant about it. But in retrospect, due to the sexual abuse I was experiencing by my father, I had subconsciously made a decision to not be violated by other men, and that any sexual contact had to be with a clear "Yes" from me.

No, I was not going to let this happen and I didn't. I blocked my breasts with my arm and pushed his hand away gently, but firmly.

And that was the end of the very brief romantic advance from George.

Looking back, I am amazed I set this boundary in the face of losing my first love. I felt very strongly about this and was willing to lose a potential romantic relationship with George in order to keep that boundary.

In high school, in addition to French, Latin and Spanish, Russian was offered as an experiment. George chose to take Russian and he later became a U.S. diplomat and was sent to Russia.

Over the years, I thought often about George until one day, about two years ago, I Googled him, and found out that unfortunately, he was in a wheelchair with a rare disease. His wife is his caretaker. I am so grateful that I didn't end up being the caretaker for anyone, even my first love.

Henry, My First Husband

I was 16 when I met Henry through my friend Monica, with whom I worked in the hospital kitchen. Henry was Monica's boyfriend's best friend. Henry needed a date for his senior prom. Monica and her boyfriend arranged for Henry and me to meet one evening after our hospital shift. After the second time of hanging out, Henry and I began to like each other. I attended his senior prom and we had a good time.

Henry and I dated, fell in love, got married and moved to Berkeley together so I could attend my Master's program. Henry and I had lots of fun. We both had a knack for seeing the humor in life and we laughed a lot. He was a talented jazz guitarist and pianist. He'd had a band in college that had many successful gigs.

After I graduated from Berkeley, and I had a good-paying job in the managed care field, Henry and I bought a condo just north of Berkeley. On weekends we loved to go to San Francisco to one of the many jazz venues and listen to fabulous music from some of the best musicians in the business. I was in heaven and to this day, one of my favorite things to do is to go to a jazz club to listen to some excellent music. One of my fondest memories with Henry was listening to him practice the piano in our home. I still miss it.

When we moved to Berkeley, after a few short-term jobs, Henry found a day job as a recruiter for a college in the Bay Area. His territory included Southern California and Alaska and he was on the road a lot. While on the road, he began drinking more than I was comfortable with, and he became quite distant. I believed he was in total denial about the drinking. I knew what having an addiction to alcohol looked like because, in addition to being a sex addict, my father was also an alcoholic, albeit a functioning one.

I loved Henry and yet I was not OK with his drinking, nor his inability to communicate his feelings. At the same time I was pondering how to leave the marriage, Henry had an emotional affair with one of the women he was working with. We were both thinking about leaving the marriage. I, however, was the one to broach the subject.

An Unexpected Promotion

Within a few days of deciding I needed to take some action about my marriage, a "miracle" happened. My company had purchased a health plan based in Connecticut. The current Chief Operating Officer (COO) had forged his credentials and they wanted to replace him immediately. My closest friend at work, the executive assistant to the president, called me and asked if I would be interested in moving to Connecticut to be the COO of the new Northeast region.

I was very interested! That same night, I received another call, this time from the president himself, offering me the position, pending the approval of the Connecticut leadership team. He told me not to tell anyone until he let my boss know that I would be leaving my current position.

Within three weeks, Henry and I split our belongings and filed for divorce. I packed, said goodbye to my many friends and made arrangements for my move to Connecticut.

Completion with Henry

Despite what family and friends advised, Henry and I decided not to hire a divorce attorney and instead filed the papers ourselves. We divided our assets before we filed the papers so the court would have nothing to decide.

I received our condo and Henry got both of our cars and most of the furniture. I was starting over in a new state, so this worked for me. Since the filing fee was $75 at that time, it cost Henry and me $37.50 each to get divorced. I am so very grateful for our love and maturity in divorcing in a graceful way.

A few years ago, Henry called me to apologize for how badly he had treated me during our marriage. Quite honestly, I was a little shocked because since our marriage ended, I have only remembered the good things we shared. I am grateful for my silver lining lens as it keeps me from having any regrets. I believe this positive lens continues to contribute to my feeling young and vital.

Paul, My Great Love

After Henry and I filed for divorce and I left for Connecticut, I lived some particularly happy years. I was enjoying professional success and I was experiencing a great romance. Soon after I arrived in the Northeast, I was asked to be a member of the local chamber of commerce board of directors. I became the vice president of the board. The president was a man named Paul.

Paul and I began dating. He had a fabulous sense of humor and we had lots of fun. We traveled well together. One of my best memories with Paul was when we vacationed on St. Barths, a gorgeous French island with many secluded beaches. We spent many hours on the nude beach and in the water. It felt like heaven.

One of the fun games that we played on St. Barths was to speak French to one other. Paul spoke fluent French and I had taken French from third grade through sophomore year in college and I was pleased to have recall of the language once I got back into it. What happy and delightful memories!

Paul and I fell in love. I was so happy when I was with him. He is 21 years older than I am and it did not bother me. In fact, about a year after we were dating, I asked Paul to marry me. He promptly said no, and I was crushed.

His reasoning was that I may want to have kids someday and he did not, and he also believed that our age difference would be a concern for me in the future. He was right. I am 66 and he is now 87. I am a vibrant, healthy woman and I would not want to be slowed down in any way since I feel as if I am just coming into the prime of my life. Thank you, Paul, for your wisdom.

In retrospect, I am sure that Paul was a father figure to me. When we were making love, I sometimes had vague flashbacks to the sexual encounters with my father. I found out many months after we started dating that Paul had a daughter who died in his arms. I believe he was unconsciously trying to recreate his relationship with his daughter. Despite the psychology of it all, we had an awesome time together.

When I left for Pittsburgh for the CEO position, it was challenging to maintain a long-distance relationship with Paul. It felt as if I was more willing to try than he, and after several months in Pittsburgh, we were no longer a couple.

Paul was the true love of my life. Even as I write these words, I feel emotional as I know we "got" one another. In addition to our age difference, we had other differences, particularly politically. I wonder how that would have played out if we had stayed together.

Harold, The Charming Narcissist

I met Harold while I lived on the island of Kauai. He is handsome, intelligent, and oh so charming.

Harold and I were introduced by a mutual friend almost immediately upon my arrival on the island. He is a coach and musician, two professions that attract me most, and here were both in one handsome man. I thought I had hit the jackpot. I was in a "relationship" with him for two of my four and a half years on the island.

I put "relationship" in quotes because Harold believed we were only friends. However, each time we got together, we spent hours and hours talking about both our professional and personal lives, in intimate detail. When he came to my house, we talked into the wee hours of the morning.

As I look back on my relationship with Harold, I know it was not all one-sided. Just like a significant other, Harold relied on me for mental, emotional and spiritual support. He shared his deepest secrets and his deepest fears with me. And I was always the supportive "partner" when he did.

One of the reasons we got together often was because we were creating a retreat together. The retreat was originally Harold's idea and he asked me to be involved, so I had an agreement with him to facilitate some sessions and to enroll some of my clients to participate.

The truth is that I did this with the intention of becoming closer to him. That mission was accomplished. We became great friends and I would say emotionally attached. I know I was. I fell in love with him, or more accurately, I fell in love with the fantasy of what we might become. What I know for sure is that we had good times together.

One night when we went to a concert together on the west side of the island, I was finally able to see things more clearly. The performer was a talented slack key guitarist and it was a sold-out show. The audience included many of my friends who were hoping this would be the night when Harold finally turned the relationship in the romantic direction.

As soon as we sat down in the old theater with cozy seats, Harold leaned over to me and said, "Let's snuggle" and I responded, "You know I would not mind that at all." Harold immediately realized what he had said and for the rest of the night became as energetically and physically distant from me as possible. And for the most part, he stopped speaking to me for the rest of our time at the concert.

After the concert, Harold ignored me. When he interacted with the star musician, I took a picture of the two of them, but Harold never asked if I wanted a picture taken as well. My dear friend

Patrick noticed what was happening and immediately swooped in and took a picture of me with the guitarist.

The next day, when I realized the reality of what had transpired the night before, I wrote an email to Harold expressing what I had observed regarding his behavior, how I felt hurt and disrespected, and that it was not OK with me. I heard from him several days later, and he simply said his behavior was not intentional. And that was the end of our "relationship."

I was finally able to see the truth, which is that Harold is the classic definition of a narcissistic — it was *all* about him. There wasn't anything that wasn't about him.

I have only spoken to Harold one time since then. That was after a heavy flood on Kauai when his home was damaged. He called and said, since the disaster, he had been thinking about all the people that matter to him. Evidently I was one of them, although he never said that directly.

What I know is that I am done being in relationships with narcissistic personalities. My father was a classic case, and he was also charming. For 33 years in a row, he was elected president of a local union for people in the graphic arts. Yes, the man that I have described in these pages was popular.

In my father's case, it was also all about himself and all about puffing up his ego. No matter what I did, said, or was being, I was never going to get the approval and acknowledgement from my father that, for much of my life, I craved. He did not have the capacity to provide that for me.

Chapter Nine: Community and Trust

Yearning for Community

During my time in La Jolla, I did a lot of business networking and was able to make friends, but what I yearned for most was a supportive, loving community of intimate friends.

At the end of April 2014, I came home to a note on my apartment door announcing that in 30 days my rent would go up significantly. If I was going to leave before the rent increased, I needed to give my 30-day notice the following day. Alrighty then, choice time.

Although I didn't know where I would be going, I knew it was time to leave. I felt complete with my time in La Jolla and gave notice I was moving out.

Unconditional Love and Trust in Paradise

I put my belongings in storage and left for three weeks for Kauai to feel into whether I wanted to move there. Ever since that visit with my grandma as a teenager, I had always felt that I would spend at least a few years on this Hawaiian island that felt like home. I had visited Kauai many times since my first trip and the calling to stay for a while longer was getting louder.

I loved my three weeks on The Garden Island, which is Kauai's nickname. I met lots of interesting people and I could see myself living there. But I was scared to make the leap.

Well, the Universe took care of my hesitancy. Upon my return to Southern California, while couch-surfing with generous friends, I could not find a place to live. I thought I wanted to live north of La Jolla and began apartment hunting up the coast. There were long waiting lists to get into any decent apartment along the shore.

A couple weeks into my apartment search, I had a session with my trusted healer, and what came through her from my Guidance was that nothing was going to work out housing-wise because I was "meant" to go to Kauai. Over the years, I have learned to trust my Guidance, and it did feel like it was time to live on Kauai.

And so, with two suitcases and a laptop, I moved to Kauai on August 13, 2014, and started my beautiful tropical island adventure. Interestingly, within the first week on island my Guidance told me I would only be there for about four years, and to take full advantage of my experience. That knowing gave me an opportunity to squeeze every ounce out of my Pacific island experience.

On Kauai I developed the most loving, supportive, intimate group of friends I'd ever had. It felt *so* good. Living on a small, rural island in the middle of the Pacific Ocean really made it easier for me to find my "peeps."

Some of the many things I loved about these friends included how they spontaneously invited me to join them for events they knew I would like, and reached out to me whenever they energetically felt I might need them. I especially loved how they listened to me, always without judgment, no matter what topic I was talking about.

I counted on these dear friends to be there for me consistently — and they were. I felt unconditional love from them, and can honestly say this was the first time I ever felt unconditionally loved. It was such a contrast from my upbringing.

While on the island, I participated in some creative adventures I never imagined I would have the opportunity to do. The one that stands out is that with the help of two dear friends, Reverends Rita and Patrick, the Co-Spiritual Directors of the Center for Spiritual Living Kauai, I wrote three one-woman shows and performed them in front of a live audience. What a thrill! I was high for days after each performance.

Another highlight from this island experience is that I spent a year taking courses in the Science of Mind philosophy founded by Ernest Holmes. Reverends Rita and Patrick were the teachers for these classes, and I learned so much from them. After a year in these classes, I was asked to be on the board of trustees for the center. I accepted and was thrilled to be able to contribute my governance and business skills to this expanding organization.

My biggest learning from my Science of Mind classes and board participation was to trust, *for real,* that Spirit has my back. I had been working on this trust issue my whole life, but my trust grew from merely being a good concept to completely embodying it.

The result is that I no longer worry. Given my history, this is a *big* deal. I know and trust that I will always be taken care of, no matter what. *This allows me a source of freedom and joy I never thought possible.*

With all this goodness happening on Kauai, how did I know that it was time to leave? I felt it energetically.

Kauai is a gorgeous island, and it is a small isolated place. I could have seen myself staying there if I were retired, but retirement is not yet on my radar. I was feeling as if I had expanded to the outer limits of what Kauai could offer me.

Move to Denver

As I began contemplating what was next, I was introduced to a program to enhance my skills in writing, speaking and entrepreneurship. It called to me and I enrolled.

I went through the freebie package and signed up for the next offer that included a three-day live event in Denver in September 2018. On the third day of this event I decided to join the yearlong program being offered. I also decided to move to Denver so I would not have to travel back and forth from Kauai for the in-person intensives that would be held in the Denver area.

The decision to leave the most nurturing place I had ever lived was not an easy one. It felt like a decision between staying with my current status quo or expanding into my next level of contribution in the world. I have always had a strong desire to grow and expand, so why stop now?

My decision to move shocked some dear friends, but I knew I could count on their loving support no matter what I chose to do. I miss these dear friends now, love knowing I can visit them whenever I choose, and with today's technology we remain in close touch. I really don't have the words to convey how good it feels to still have them in my life.

At 64 years old, this move was a symbol of who I have become: a badass serial entrepreneur and lifelong learner who is confident enough to recreate a loving, supportive community of friends no matter where I relocate.

At the end of November 2018, I flew to Los Angeles, picked up my Honda named Olive (which had just crossed the Pacific) from the Long Beach dock and began my road trip from Southern California to Denver, with stops along the way to visit old friends and some of my coaching clients. As I write this from Denver, opportunities continue to open for me.

Chapter Ten: Powerful Completions

Divorcing Gupta

During the seven years that Gupta was not working, his mother, who lived in India, became ill and needed open-heart surgery. She did not have insurance. Being the eldest son, Gupta was expected to pay for most of his mother's operation. But Gupta was not earning any money, so it fell on my shoulders to do so. We transferred thousands of dollars in cash to his mother's account in India to pay for her heart operation. Fortunately, the operation went well.

Several months later, Gupta's mother had another request. Her longtime live-in servant's daughter was getting married and needed money for a dowry. I was asked to provide that dowry.

There was no way I was going to pay for my mother-in-law's servant's daughter's dowry!

I do not believe in the dowry tradition and the subjugation of women as it is propagated in India and many other parts of the world. I needed to draw the line somewhere. My answer was an emphatic "No!" I left Gupta to deal with his mother on this one.

Actually, I had been supporting Gupta's mother for years by sending cash to India when she asked Gupta for it, which meant that I was supporting her servant as well, which I suppose is what gave her the idea that I would surely say "Yes" to the dowry.

When I married Gupta, I never imagined I would be the sole breadwinner for not only myself, but for Gupta, his mother, and her servant, which also meant the servant's family! *No wonder I felt burdened and exhausted.*

A couple of years after the "servant dowry" episode, I ended my marriage to Gupta, and although it was just as amicable as with Henry, it was a bit more challenging. The trickiest part was that Gupta had a good thing going with me being his provider and he wasn't fond of giving that up.

He had a female friend (actually most of Gupta's friends were female — I called them "the harem," which he enjoyed, being the guru he thought himself to be) who decided that upon our divorce, I would owe Gupta alimony. I needed to deal with this issue very skillfully.

Here is how I handled it: I gave Gupta whatever possessions he desired. He ended up with more than 60 percent of the furniture, artwork, household goods, etc. We sold the house before we filed for divorce and split the proceeds. This was fortuitous for both of us because Gupta and I had completed a bankruptcy just over a year prior to this. In the bankruptcy, we had been able to keep our home and our cars.

The bankruptcy had been a huge emotional issue for me. I was clear that it was our own actions that had caused the need to file for bankruptcy. Gupta had not worked for seven years, "we" were supporting his mother in India, and we did not scale down our lifestyle. When I look at it in retrospect, it seems bankruptcy was the inevitable outcome.

I vividly remember this scene in the living room of our Scottsdale home: I created a ceremony in which Gupta and I cut up our many credit cards that we could no longer use. I was sobbing, and clear that I was committed to never creating this situation again.

Final Completion with Gupta

A couple of years ago Gupta had a stroke. I was living on Kauai at the time. He got in touch with me immediately. He wanted me to let others know about his stroke, and so I did.

After a few more calls, the real reason for him getting in touch with me came to light. He had decided that since I had not re-married, and neither had he, he expected I would leave Hawaii and come to Arizona to take care of him.

You have got to be kidding me!

This expectation was *so* Gupta. He assumed I would do anything he wanted because, of course, he was entitled to that as my guru. I let him know that since we had been divorced for 13 years, it was time to be complete with our relationship and that I wished him the very best. I am no longer in communication with him.

Glorious Gift From a Car Accident

When I was 53 and living in Seattle, one of the most dramatic events of my life took place. It was late on a Friday afternoon, I was driving, and Candy was in the front passenger seat. We were entering the bridge to get off Mercer Island to go to the movies and were hit from behind by an inexperienced teenage driver. Candy screamed. I was calm as I always am in crisis situations. I left my beloved lime green Volkswagen Beetle on the road for the police to handle so I could go to the hospital with Candy.

My car was totaled. Both of us had significant recovery time with whiplash, and neck and back injuries. The accident caused me to have a series of chiropractic, massage and energy healing sessions three times a week, which took a great deal of time and focus. I was very intentional about getting better as quickly as possible, and did so in less than a year.

One of the great things that resulted from these healing sessions was that some of the unhealthy structural issues in my back, that were from long before the car accident, began to heal. As my somatic massage practitioner began to work on my back and neck, I could feel the "unwinding" happening internally. The bodily results of the trauma and drama of my childhood began to heal.

I am so grateful for the skill of my somatic practitioner, who is a good friend to this day, and to my car insurance for paying for this healing. This was a precious gift from the accident and from the Universe.

"You've Done Nothing Wrong"

For the past 33-plus years I have been proud of being an encouraging and skillful coach. My clients thrive. There is one memorable exception.

One of my new friends from my New Thought church in San Diego, asked me to coach her son, who was in his early 20s. She framed it like this: John was having trouble deciding what he wanted to do next and he was a little down.

I talked with John, who indeed seemed quite directionless, and I agreed to coach him. We had one coaching session, meeting for coffee halfway between our respective homes. We sat outside for privacy.

John talked about a love issue and about the next possible career moves he was mulling over. As I do in all my coaching sessions, I asked him lots of questions, and was very encouraging. After our time together, he said he felt better, and he seemed to have shifted to a much more positive mood. We set up time to meet for our next session.

As is my practice, I text my clients the day before to confirm their appointment. I did that with John for our second appointment, including a reminder to bring payment. He texted back and confirmed he was meeting me for our appointment the next morning.

And then, the most horrific thing happened. That evening I received a text from John's mother that John had taken his life.

I felt as if I had been punched in the stomach. I became nauseous and off balance. I tried reaching out to my two healers and a friend from church. None of them were available right away. The first few hours after this news were hellish.

What did I do wrong? Why had I not seen this coming?

My mind raced on and on with doubts and questions.

One thing kept haunting me: I knew John was struggling with having no income and that is why his mother was paying for my services. Had I created the tipping point for John by asking him about payment in my text?

A few days later there was an evening healing session at my church. It is a beautiful service where the sanctuary is filled with candlelight. All those in attendance meditate together. I decided this was the perfect place for me.

As I sat there in the sanctuary, I went through many emotions. As soon as my mind had settled down, I felt John's presence from the other side and heard him say to me, *"It was my choice. You have done nothing wrong. You have done nothing wrong."* I tuned in further and could feel that John was energetically very near. After assuring me several more times that I had done nothing wrong, he told me he needed to leave me to be by his mother's side.

And so, after a lifetime of feeling as if I was always "doing something wrong" due to my sexual abuse history, I finally understood deeply that I had done nothing wrong regarding John. And all those other times I thought I had done something wrong, I had not. It had just been a tape running in my head.

John's words offered me life-altering relief!

The dread of "having done something wrong" has never returned. I am so very grateful to John for being the angel who set me free.

Last Encounters with My Father

The last time I saw my father in his home was about 13 years ago. It was my younger sister's 50th birthday. She wanted to visit my parents in Florida, where they lived, before we four sisters went to Disney World to spend a few days together.

On our first day there, I was in the kitchen with my father, excitedly sharing with him about my new adventures in the Seattle area. His response to my enthusiasm was a long diatribe about something he was doing. He ended his long talk with, "That ought to knock you down a peg or two."

Throughout my lifetime, he'd used that phrase often with me. His other favorite "advice" was "Don't get too big for your britches." These phrases had a huge effect on me, and I may still be working out some remnants of these hurtful admonishments.

The last time I saw my father was when I decided to go to Florida about a year later when he was in the hospital for a heart operation. I knew it would be the last time I would see him and I didn't want to have any regrets.

It was a very emotional encounter. I told him I loved him, and thanked him for all the things I learned from him. I assume he thought I learned only "good things," but mostly what I learned from him was how *not* to be.

My father lived for several more years, but I never visited him again. I was complete.

My Surprising Guardian Angel

My father died while I was living in La Jolla. For years, thoughts of him made me feel protective of myself.

Several months ago, I was having a potent healing session with one of my colleagues, and at the end of our session, she said my dad was present, and he wanted to be my guardian angel. I had felt this for a long time but had resisted, for I did not trust his motivation. Now, with the healer, it was the first time I felt as if I was able to allow him to do that for me. I believe that my father, or my father's soul, wants to make amends, and this is his way of doing it. I completely forgave him.

What I know for sure is that I deserve guardian angels who help me when I need it. I also know that I deserve a life of freedom and joy, which I am very grateful to be living! I wouldn't change any experiences in my life, for each one has made me who I am.

I believe I will live for many years to come on this earthly plane and that I will continue to evolve into my best ever me.

Epilogue

Since writing this book, an extraordinary thing happened. While participating in a daylong workshop led by a medium, a person who talks with those who have passed on, my beloved maternal grandmother came through one of the mediums in attendance with messages for me.

Grandma Elaine had a lot to say! She wanted me to know that she knew I was being abused as a child, and that she had tried to intervene, but both my parents denied it, despite what she called "evidence." My grandma also wanted to convey that she was very sorry she didn't pursue it further, and that I should have been included in the discussions with my parents.

She said that she loved me very much, was always with me and that she would be the first to greet me on "the other side," although that was many years away.

This validation from my grandma meant so much to me. It made me feel even more sure of sharing my story for those who may benefit by it.

As I look back on what I have written about my life, certain themes emerge: shame, lack of worthiness, jealousy, blame, denial, hope, optimism, curiosity, courage, unstoppable life force, resilience, humor and trust.

I spent many years feeling like a victim with arrogance smeared on top of it.

I did not develop self-confidence until I was many years into my internal self-evolvement journey. In order to mask my lack of self-confidence, I would act overly confident, with a dose of arrogance for good measure.

Toward the end of my marriage with Henry, when we were living in a condo in Northern California, Henry was becoming more and more distant and less and less communicative. I tried everything I knew how to do to get him to open up to me, without success. I felt helpless and definitely like a victim.

One day during this period, I came home late from work (as usual), stopped at the mailbox to pick up the mail, and was accosted from behind. I swung around and saw a young man fleeing down the street with my purse. I started to run after him, but he was way too fast. I heard Spirit say "Stop, be safe."

As I walked into the condo, I was very upset. Yet this was a huge wake-up call, for I believe the outside world reflects one's inside world. I was being shown that I had been thinking, feeling and being a victim. No wonder I was accosted.

I made a clear decision that, from that moment forward, I was unwilling to live in victim mode. I began actively working on this issue in therapy and my intense personal development work.

My deep commitment not to live as a victim is the single-most important thing that propelled me beyond my history of sexual and emotional abuse. I practice and demonstrate this commitment to myself in big and small ways daily. One of my techniques is to speak up for myself with clarity and kindness many times a day.

I also have developed an amazing life-changing tool to see others' points of view, i.e. to see an issue from *their* world view. I practice this often so that even when I am in pain or hurting from what someone has said or done, I am nearly always able to see the situation from their vantage point, which alleviates the hurt much more quickly than it might otherwise.

This doesn't mean I agree with their perspective, or that I am letting go of my own viewpoint, but it allows me to practice being the compassionate person I am.

I have become very good at forgiveness. I have forgiven my perpetrators and those who did not protect me. Having forgiven such extreme violations, I now find it easier to forgive others for less egregious acts.

Most importantly, in order to live a full, rich, healthy, happy and contributing life, I also have forgiven myself.

I had done a ton of self-forgiveness prior to my client's taking of his life, but his direct words of "You've done nothing wrong" helped to dissipate any remaining vestiges of self-flagellation.

Forgiving myself has been an active practice of mine for many years, and I believe it will continue throughout this lifetime and beyond.

I believe that self-forgiveness is directly related to loving one's self. As I forgive myself for things in the present, I know that it is a courageous act of self-love. And as I love myself more and more each day, I am expanding my capacity for joy.

Perhaps what assists me most to stay in a positive mindset much of the time is that I believe and trust in Spirit. I know, beyond a shadow of a doubt, that I am safe, and I am well taken care of.

I believe that there are no accidents, meaning that whatever is occurring or has occurred is for my learning and Highest Good. Because of this belief, I live my life with no regrets — not even regarding the horrific things that happened to me as a child and teenager.

My friend Sydney believes that this may be my last lifetime on this planet and that I am getting all my last lessons in before I move on to whatever is next in the Universal experience. I don't know if this is true or not, but what I do know is that I feel more freedom and joy with each passing day.

Contemplative Questions

As a seasoned coach and through my own self-evolvement work, I have found that open-ended journaling questions are a beautiful way to integrate what one has read or learned.

The questions that follow are related to potent themes in this book and when answered, may open new realms of healing and an expanded awareness of one's self.

I suggest that you answer each with your "gut reaction," with what is at the top of your heart and mind. This intuitive response will be the answer most closely connected to your soul. Enjoy the process!

When have you felt confident and assured?
When have you felt not as worthy as you would prefer to feel?

What is your definition of resilience?
Do you consider yourself a resilient person?

*Do you consider yourself to be
generally optimistic or pessimistic?
Why do you think this is?*

Are you a curious person?
What piques your curiosity?

Do you consider yourself to be a courageous person?
Why or why not?

Do you appreciate a good sense of humor?
Do you think you have a good sense of humor?

Do you have an innate or developed sense of trust that the Universe has your back?

When have you taken a "leap of faith?"
Have you taken one rarely or often?